The Yes/No Quali

The Yes/No Quality of Dreams

David Robilliard

The Bad Press

Published in 2000
by The Bad Press,
PO Box 76,
Manchester,
M21 8HJ.
www.thebadpress.co.uk

ISBN 1 903160 04 9

1 3 5 7 9 2 4 6 8

All rights reserved.
Copyright Chris Hall, 2000.

A CIP catalogue record for this book
is available from The British Library.
Cover photo by Peter Wright.
Back photo by Dan Lepard.
Inside photo by Mark Baker.
Author as a child circa 1958.
Copyright Jayne Robilliard.
Drawings by David Robilliard.
Copyright Chris Hall, 2000.
Book designed by Robert Cochrane.
Grateful thanks to Chris Hall,
Catherine Hollens, John Hollens
and Gary Parkinson, without whom...

Printed by
The Arc and Throstle Press Limited,
Nanholme Mill, Shaw Wood Road,
Todmorden, Lancs, OL14 6DA.

CONTENTS

ACID INDIGESTION	09
SPLITTING HEADACHE	10
OUT OF ORDER POETRY	11
LIFE IN PROGRESS	12
YOU SAID GOODBYE	13
THE LIQUIDS THAT KEEP YOU...	14
YOU RADDLED OLD BAT	15
DOING NOTHING DAYS	16
CHINESE WHISPERS	17
GET THAT SLUT OFF STAGE	18
SAME OLD STORY	19
CASUAL COOEY CONVERSATION	20
MODERN TACK	21
ALL THE HAPPY COUPLES	22
BEYOND SELF CONTROL	23
PARANOIA NEVER DIES	24
THE FORMER OCCUPANT	25
A LET DOWN	26
WOULD I?	27
NO	28
AND WHEN...	29
THE FIRST BIRD	30
EATING OUT	31
YOUR BODY	32
LOOK ELSEWHERE	33
LISTLESS	34
FULFILMENT OF DESIRE	35
YOUR LIFE	36
INTENSE DESIRE	37
SCREAMING FUCKIN' CRYING	38

SONGS OF SWINGING YEARS	39
SINCERE ORGASMS	40
HUMAN TRAITS	41
I WISH I HAD A BIT OF SPARE LIKE YOU	42
NEXT DAY	43
FATE ACCOMPANYING	44
I CAN'T REMEMBER THE FEATURES OF	45
DEAD BODIES IN THE DEBRIS	46
2ND BEST	47
POLITE BYSTANDERS	48
WHAT'S NEW?	49
THE TIMES I'VE GONE HOME ALONE	50
THE NATURE OF THE BEAST	51
I AM A LIMITED EDITION	53
VISCOUS LICKOUT	54
TRUE LOVE	55
3 POSSIBILITIES	56
NO PARTY	57
FEEBLE FARTS	58
ONE MINUTE WONDER	59
THE ONLY OCCASION	60
COME AGAIN	61
GLOBAL	62
NOT TO	63
DON'T MISS THE TRAIN	64

For Gilbert and George.

ACID INDIGESTION

Definitely no 'Ecstasy'
involved there.

SPLITTING HEADACHE

Cracking headache.
Thumping headache.
Still,
it's better than
getting a migraine.
Innit?

OUT OF ORDER POETRY

You are just settling
down to sleep when you
think of something to write down.
You think
'Oh it's so clear and simple,
 I'm bound to remember it in the morning.'
And of course you wake up with a blank.

LIFE IN PROGRESS

Eat me out of house and home,
and the you can piss off
and leave me alone.

MOVING AROUND

You said 'Goodbye'
with a beautiful smile.

THE LIQUIDS THAT KEEP YOU FROM SLEEP

Also keep you alive.

YOU RADDLED OLD BAT!

Don't worry.
We all come to that!

DOING NOTHING DAYS

Are very similar
to nothing doing days.

CHINESE WHISPERS

When you feel like there's a ton of bricks
falling on your head,
the universe trips,
acid house falls down
and ecstasy is no more,
and then you were pissed
and all the nonsense made sense,
and then you were sober
and remembered none of it.

GET THAT SLUT OFF STAGE

'Get that slut off stage!'
'That's no way to talk to your ex.'
'But that's the bottom line for all exes.'
'Not necessarily.'
'Oh well -
  GET THAT SLUT OFF STAGE!'

SAME OLD STORY

You are the only person
I want to speak to
and you're not in today,
and then there's the host
of potential partners
somewhere out in the world,
waiting for potential partners
as the sun brings another day
to the simmer, trouble is,
I can't cool down at night.

CASUAL COOEY CONVERSATION

Death doesn't wear glasses,
or make passes.
It takes everyone by storm,
turns the warm to cold,
the young to old.
Death is greedy,
but though it can't read
it helps the poor and needy.
Death is dumb
and yet stronger than the sun.
Would you like another cup of tea?

MODERN TACK

When we first came out of the sea
who'd have thought we'd have
flying rooms that go round the world,
and even to other planets?

ALL THE HAPPY COUPLES

"That's his bum chum."
"That's his tart of a wife."
"That's her shit of a husband."
"Oh look out...
   LOVELY PARTY DARLING!
   Nice to see all the happy couples."

BEYOND SELF CONTROL

Your mother wants you
to clean up your act.
She wouldn't be
any more interested in it,
just less offended,

PARANOIA NEVER DIES

People like to shoot you
out of the sky
and turn you into bogey pie.
No wonder paranoia never dies.

THE FORMER OCCUPANT

An empty pair of shoes
on the corner of the street,
I wonder what happened
to the former occupant?

A LET DOWN

"Oh you're going to one of those parties,
 you look like Batman and Robin."
"You're like Rapunzel's hair."
"What do you mean?"
"A let down."

WOULD I?

Would I fancy myself
if I was somebody else?

NO

No,
I don't think I could
Gauge your age.
I've never seen you off stage.

AND WHEN...

And when
people say to you
"I'm just..."
You know it's
a metaphor for nothing.

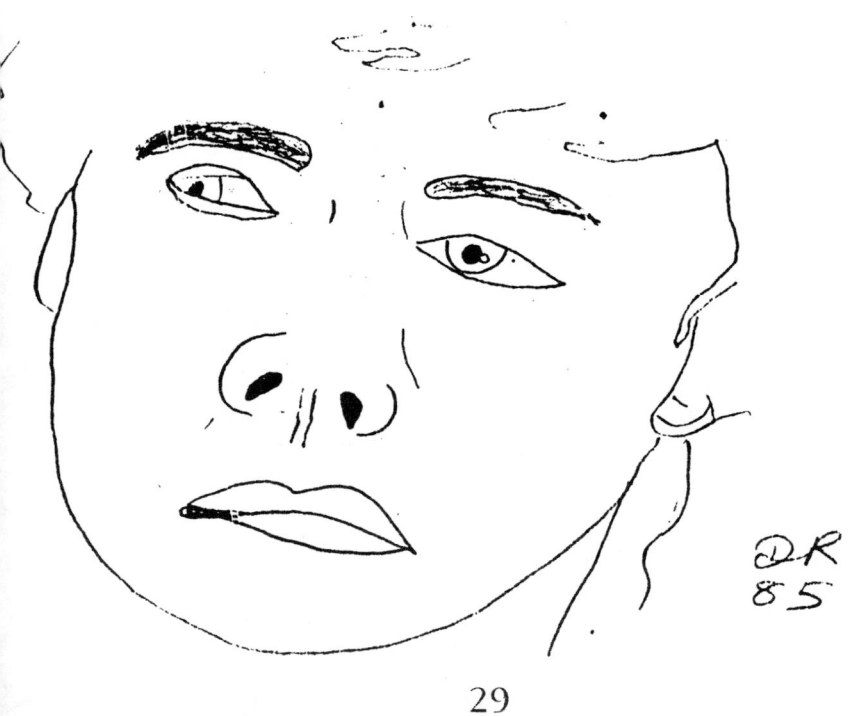

THE FIRST BIRD

The first bird sings
before the last bat
folds its wings.

EATING OUT

You're like a potato.
You'd go with anything.

YOUR BODY

Your body was found,
Twisted and broken
on the ground,
and it cost
less than a pound
to read the gory story.

LOOK ELSEWHERE

When someone
you've got designs on,
signs on
at the same time as you,
and takes no notice of you.
What can you do?

LISTLESS

There's no point
in naming the friendless,
the list would be endless.

FULFILMENT OF DESIRE

Frustrated or elated,
both are related
to the same thing.

YOUR LIFE

In and out and round about.
the story of your life;
on the front page is your sex,
your striving, your strife,
and on the back page
is your obituary.

INTENSE DESIRE

The thing that thrilled them,
was the thing that killed them.

SCREAMING FUCKIN' CRYING

Screaming fuckin' crying.
Nothing you can do
will stop you from dying.

SONGS OF THE SWINGING YEARS

Take all the romantic sadness
from all those movies that we saw,
then watch them some more.
How this music reminds me
of you darling,
our separate ways
vanish in the haze,
but deep down
the memory stays.

SINCERE ORGASMS

Our belle epoch,
we've been through
a few scenes together,
me and thee,
haven't we?
Waking up to sex...
what do you expect?
Lonely days and nights
reaching out into the darkness
of nothing.

HUMAN TRAITS

Your shadow flies away
and your memory fades.

I WISH I HAD A BIT OF SPARE LIKE YOU

You two love each other so much
that no matter how many people
try to pull you apart,
it doesn't work.
You've even tried it yourselves,
and failed.

NEXT DAY

The ecstasy you shared with me
can easily be gotten elsewhere.
Still,
I feel much better
because of it.

FATE ACCOMPANYING

It was awful,
I was putting my knickers on
and there was somebody's
false teeth in 'em.

I CAN'T REMEMBER THE FEATURES

of the person
I'm about
to tell you
about.

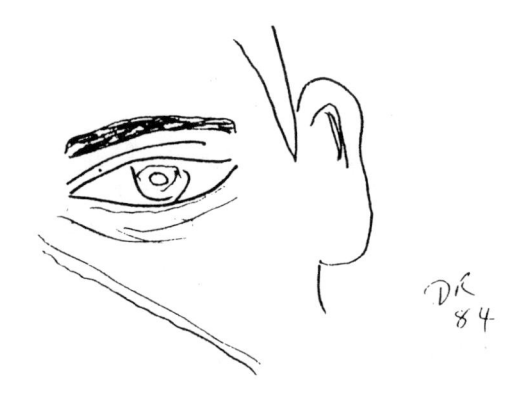

THE DISCO WHO'S WHO

It's not Noah's Ark,
but there they go
two by two,
sometimes they don't
and sometimes they do.

DEAD BODIES IN THE DEBRIS

Great minds of each age
served to you on a micro-page,
Will the viruses chase us through space,
or are there new threats
apart from lack of air?

2ND BEST

It only takes a second
to laugh or cry,
or be bored,
or die.

POLITE BYSTANDERS

There I was
sitting on a chair
next to your parents,
feeling exposed.
A hairs-breadth away
from being ourselves.

WHAT'S NEW?

The one you want
don't want you.

THE TIMES I'VE GONE HOME ALONE

Have usually been less disastrous
than the times I haven't.

THE NATURE OF THE BEAST

The people you like the least
are the most persistent.
The people you like the most
are the most evasive.

I AM A LIMITED EDITION

So are you.

VISCOUS LICKOUT

The ultimate beauty,
lips on glass
of the car window
that just passed.

TRUE LOVE (2)

"I never believed you existed."
"But you hoped."
"True."

3 POSSIBILITIES

Above ground.
Ground.
Below Ground.

NO PARTY

No party is complete
without
someone nice to meet.

FEEBLE FARTS

Don't you think those people
who quote something you've said
as their own
just a few minutes later,
to you
or in front of you,
are feeble farts?

ONE MINUTE WONDER

Oh My God!
An Angel just walked in.
Surprise, Surprise.
Somebody blocked my view
and away you flew.

THE ONLY OCCASION

The only occasion
you won't be cruising
at dear,
is your own funeral.

COME AGAIN

Reincarnation is just another way
of getting into somebody else's pants.

GLOBAL

We may all live on the globe,
but we're not all having a ball.

NOT TO

You're young enough not to mind.
I'm old enough not to care.

DON'T MISS THE TRAIN

The person you desire leaves
and you put the record
back in its sleeve,
a dusty old jazz record
you got out of the attic.
You finish your glass of wine
and dash out to the party.
You face your own reality.
Your shadow never overtakes you.